Original title:
A Season of Wonder and Light

Copyright © 2024 Creative Arts Management OÜ
All rights reserved.

Author: Lorenzo Barrett
ISBN HARDBACK: 978-9916-94-064-8
ISBN PAPERBACK: 978-9916-94-065-5

Threads of Sunshine

The sunshine weaves through trees,
Like cats chasing after a sneeze.
Jellybeans dance on the lawn,
As bees buzz where the grass is drawn.

Kites are tangled in the breeze,
Chasing squirrels like happy fleas.
Children giggle, rolling down,
While ice cream melts and sticks the crown.

Silhouettes in the Glow

Shadows play games on the ground,
Squirrels in hats pass around.
Laughter echoes on the street,
As toes in flip-flops tap to the beat.

Moonlight twinkles in your drink,
While fireflies buzz and wink.
Dancing with shadows, we jig,
Making shadows of each big wig.

The Breath of Spring

Blossoms tickle the nose, oh my!
Hiccups from laughter fill the sky.
Daisies wear hats made of dew,
While bunnies hop and play peekaboo.

The wind whispers silly jokes,
As tulips sway like little blokes.
Chirping birds tweet with great flair,
While frogs bounce around without a care.

Heartbeats in the Light

Sunbeams rumble like a drum,
Chasing after a chocolate crumb.
Puppies spin in circles cute,
While daisies dance in a silly suit.

Juggling clouds in the blue sky,
Acrobatic squirrels zip and fly.
Laughter echoes through the park,
As fireflies twinkle in the dark.

Prisms of Possibility

Rainbows dance in the air,
Unicorns everywhere,
Jumping on clouds with glee,
Sipping tea from a tree.

Butterflies wear silly hats,
Dancing with giggling cats,
While llamas do a jig,
In the shade of a twig.

Socks on hands, hats on toes,
Tickling the sunlit rose,
Jellybeans float on by,
Winking at the lazy sky.

Marshmallow clouds drift apart,
Checkered breezes start to dart,
With every twist and turn,
New surprises we discern.

Reflections of Joy

Mirrors laughing with delight,
Shimmering in the sunlight,
Ducks in bow ties quack and sing,
Joyous tales that make us spring.

Fishing for giggles in the pond,
With gummy worms of which we're fond,
Jumping frogs wear silly smiles,
Croak their tunes for a few miles.

Twirling bright in neon shoes,
Pigs in pom-poms join the news,
With every hop and playful jest,
Laughter bubbles in our chest.

Tickling the beams of the sun,
Silly games for everyone,
With a wink and a funny face,
We join the craziest race.

A Symphony of Light

Chirping ants with tambourines,
Dancing under the pine machines,
Crickets scratch on their guitars,
Birds kick up clouds of candy bars.

Sunbeams conduct the playful breeze,
Each note sways like giggling trees,
Frogs in top hats play the keys,
A symphony that aims to please.

Light shines through a silly chime,
Behind the mushrooms, tiny mimes,
They tickle the shadows of the night,
Creating a show of pure delight.

Fireflies dance in circles round,
Their flickering laughter is profound,
In this concert, we all partake,
Music made for fun's own sake.

Luminous Landscapes

Glowing paths of jelly light,
Wobble through the starry night,
Twirling trees with sprinkles bright,
Guide us on our silly flight.

Dancing hills with candy trails,
Chocolate rivers, marshmallow sails,
Squirrel conductors wave their paws,
Cheering on the funny flaws.

Each shadow hides a joke or two,
Where giggles sprout like morning dew,
In this land of light and cheer,
Every chuckle will appear.

Luminous jokes bloom and grow,
On a background of starry glow,
So bring your grin and lend your ear,
To the wacky world of laughter here.

Infinite Horizons

From dawn till dusk, the giggles play,
Silly clouds dance in the light of day.
Butterflies flutter, they can't keep still,
Winking at flowers, what a thrill!

A squirrel on a swing, oh what a sight,
Chasing his tail in joyful delight.
Jumping through puddles with a splashy cheer,
Nature's slapstick show, come gather near!

Nature's Morning Glow

In the morning's glow, the sun jumps high,
Birds in bowties, oh my, oh my!
Rabbits in shades, sipping tea by the stream,
Every little critter living the dream.

A rooster in boots sings a funny tune,
Dancing with daisies, under the moon.
Grasshoppers giggle, they tickle the breeze,
While daisies whisper secrets to the trees.

An Ode to Radiance

Oh radiant sun, your rays are a jest,
Making shadows play hide-and-seek with the rest.
Look at that beetle, all dressed up in spots,
Trying to impress the bees, but he's not.

The daisies are laughing, in blooming array,
As dandelions puff, they're blowing away.
A snail on a skateboard, oh, the tricks he employs,
Gliding and sliding, just making some noise!

Days of Dappled Sun

With patches of light, the day gets so bright,
Tickling the toes of shadows in flight.
Chasing a sunbeam, oh what a race,
A giggling breeze puts a smile on each face.

The trees tell tales, with branches all waving,
While ants hold a parade, oh how they're behaving!
Joy in each moment, from dawn to the night,
Nature's laughter ringing, a pure delight!

Breezes of Bliss

The wind tickles trees, oh what a tease,
Dancing leaves sway with such great ease.
Squirrels prance, looking quite absurd,
Chasing their tails without a word.

Butterflies giggle in flowers bright,
Playing peek-a-boo in morning light.
Birds sing tunes that sound a bit off,
As if they're trying hard not to scoff.

Illuminated Earth

The sun winks down, a playful grin,
Leaves shimmer like they've had too much gin.
Rabbits hop around, a silly sight,
Dressed in their best for the frolicsome night.

Clouds puff up like marshmallows sweet,
A race through the sky on invisible feet.
Everyone's laughing, as shadows flip,
In this sunny dance, no one will trip!

Blossoms of Delight

Petals giggle as they start to bloom,
Wiggling and jiggling, making room.
Bees don silly hats, buzzing around,
In a honeyed world, where joy is found.

Grass blades join in with a sprightly cheer,
Whispering secrets that only they hear.
As frogs tell jokes in a croaky tone,
Their lily pad throne is a comical zone.

Dreamscapes Aglow

In the twilight hour, fireflies play,
Lighting up paths like stars gone astray.
The moon cracks jokes with a cheeky grin,
While owls hoot laughter, let the fun begin!

Dreamers wander on cloud-shaped floats,
Sailing through air in fanciful boats.
Each wave of whimsy bursts in delight,
As magic unfolds in the still of night.

Nature's Whispered Secrets

In the garden, gnomes do dance,
They wear their hats and take a chance.
A squirrel steals a bite of pie,
While butterflies gossip and skip by.

The flowers giggle, petals bright,
They poke the clouds with pure delight.
A snail plays tag— it's quite absurd,
And with a smile, the frogs concur.

The sun peeks in, a cheeky grin,
While ants hold hands and spin to win.
Each rustle is a joke, you see,
As nature shares her comedy.

Journey Through the Gleam

Bubbles float, and so do dreams,
A toaster sings with buttered beams.
Giggles leap from trees so tall,
As shadows dance and squirrels brawl.

Marshmallow clouds drift overhead,
They tease the birds, from dawn till bed.
A raccoon dons a shiny hat,
While frogs debate who's fatter, that!

Oh, don't forget the fireflies,
Who wear those tiny, twinkling ties.
They light the way for all to see,
In this joyous revelry!

Wonders of the Open Sky

The clouds are cotton candy fluff,
And rainbows think they're oh so tough.
Kites swoop low, like birds in flight,
Chasing giggles till the night.

A cat on a roof strikes a pose,
While owls craft poems in prose.
The stars waltz with a silver cheer,
As space provides its laughter here.

The sun plays peek-a-boo with glee,
While comet tails are speedy spree.
Such whimsy fills the endless air,
With chuckles floating everywhere.

Light and Laughter

A lantern winks, a joyful sight,
While shadows jiggle in the night.
The moon pulls pranks, tickles the sea,
As laughter echoes, wild and free.

Old trees share tales of days gone past,
While giggling leaves fall down so fast.
A lantern fly steals someone's hat,
And blames the wind—what's up with that?

Together, all in merry play,
The fireflies dance, a bright bouquet.
Each twinkling spark, a happy cheer,
In this bright world, we hold so dear.

Whispers of the Dawn

The sun wakes up with a yawn,
It stretches wide, oh, what a dawn!
The rooster crows, a silly sound,
While squirrels dance upon the ground.

Birds complain of their early shift,
While dewdrops play, they skip and drift.
A dog rolls over, gives a sigh,
Wishing for breakfast and pie in the sky.

Flowers greet the day with glee,
As bees buzz in a wild spree.
Butterflies laugh, doing their jig,
While ants parade with a tiny twig.

The morning's bright, the world's a show,
With giggles from the grass below.
Come join the fun, don't be shy,
In this day where silliness flies high!

Luminescent Dreams

In twilight's glow, dreams start to dance,
The fireflies wear their evening pants.
With a flicker here and a flicker there,
They twirl around in joyous air.

Moonbeams giggle, casting their light,
On sleepy cats that prowl at night.
Stars joke about their twinkling game,
While owls hoot with a laugh and a name.

Clouds drift softly, like cotton candy,
While night critters plan something dandy.
Rabbits hop in their moonlit parade,
Under the magic, their mischief is made.

So close your eyes, let laughter invade,
In dreams so bright, we'll never fade.
A night so lively, full of delight,
Where even shadows laugh at their plight!

Chasing the Golden Hour

As the sun dips low, shadows race,
Chasing hues in a lovely embrace.
Kids run wild, squealing with cheer,
While dogs join in, wiggling near.

Balloons float high, what a sight,
As giggles fill the fading light.
The ice cream truck plays a happy tune,
While kids chase it under the moon.

Lemonade stands spill over with sass,
As sticky fingers grab at the glass.
A splash of fun from the garden hose,
Turns a simple game into a prose.

So let's squeeze out each golden ray,
With laughter echoing all the way.
For in this hour, life's a treat,
As we dance on sunshine, oh what a feat!

Sprinkles of Starlight

Under the night, the world shines bright,
With sprinkles of starlight, what a sight!
The moon winks down, playing a prank,
As dreams flow out from its silvery tank.

Children wish for magic to land,
As giggles soar above the sand.
Comets race, with a whoosh and a zoom,
While hedgehogs party in the garden's bloom.

Glowworms flash in a hilarious manner,
While crickets serenade with a clamor.
Fireworks pop from every tree,
As laughter twirls, wild and free.

So embrace the night, let dreams take flight,
With sparkles of joy that feel just right.
For in this moment, no worries near,
Just funny tales and blissful cheer!

The Art of Daylight

Morning arrives with a wink,
The sun pranks the sleepy street,
Coffee cups dance and clink,
As the day jumps to its feet.

Clouds don't mind wearing a frown,
They're just shy, playing hard to get,
But soon they'll wear a golden crown,
While nature serves a bright vignette.

Birds chirp jokes from the trees,
Fleeting shadows chase the light,
Grass tickles toes with ease,
As laughter floats up in flight.

The day paints smiles everywhere,
Each moment, a colorful tease,
Whispers of joy fill the air,
The world in a funny, sweet breeze.

Celebrating the Rise

Waking up to a cheerful glow,
The sun rolls out, making friends,
It trips on a cloud, just for show,
And giggles start where the light bends.

Morning pancakes stack up high,
With syrup rivers on the side,
Toast pops up with a silly sigh,
As if it too, took a fun ride!

Tick-tock goes the playful clock,
Each second a chance to play,
Even the cuckoo likes to mock,
As time dances the day away.

Grab your hat, let's spin and prance,
Through fields where wild daisies bloom,
With laughter, we can take this chance,
To fill every corner with a room!

Flurry of Possibilities

Frosty flakes swirl on the street,
Each one a little jester's hat,
They whirl and twirl to a funny beat,
Bouncing off roofs with a splat!

Footprints stampede, a silly race,
Chasing tails of quicksilver dreams,
Laughter echoes, a jubilant space,
As kids launch snowballs, like beams!

The world dresses in white giggles,
While cocoa swirls in mugs so round,
Winter plays and softly wiggles,
While joy spreads out, all around.

What magic lies in a twinkling light,
As we dance with shadows at dusk,
Every moment, a whimsical sight,
Creating memories, sweet and brusque.

Melodies of the Moonlit Realm

The moon hums a tune, quite absurd,
As stars join in with a wink,
Night's creatures gather, not a word,
In a chorus of mischief, they blink.

Owls telling tales with a sly grin,
While raccoons conspire, all in jest,
Fireflies waltz on a breezy spin,
Twirling gently, in night's lavish vest.

Bats chuckle as they swoop and dive,
While crickets strum their shiny strings,
The air is alive, feels so alive,
In the twilight where laughter springs.

So let's sing along with the dark,
Chase shadows, let the giggles swell,
In this luminous, cheeky arc,
Where every night holds a joke to tell.

Embracing the Warmth

Sunny days and silly hats,
Squirrels dance on garden mats.
Lemonade spills, oh what a mess,
Chasing shadows in my dress.

Butterflies flit with giggling glee,
They tickle the flowers, can't you see?
The wind whispers jokes in my ear,
I burst out laughing, never fear!

Ice cream drips down fingers sweet,
A cone becomes a sticky treat.
Ticklish toes in grassy fields,
Every smile is what it yields.

So let's toast to all that's bright,
With sparkly drinks that feel just right.
Cheers to the joy on our faces,
In this warmth, we find our places.

Kaleidoscope of Joy

Colors swirl like candy canes,
Laughter buzzes in our veins.
Jumping puddles, splashing around,
Every giggle a joyful sound.

Balloons float up, up, and away,
Chasing them is the game we play.
A dog in sunglasses runs in glee,
His tail a wagging symphony.

Rainbows paint the skies at night,
With sparkly stars that tickle the light.
Each twinkling thought, a little rhyme,
Jumping between space and time.

Collecting memories in our hats,
Twirling like a bunch of brats.
Found joy dances on this shore,
In a world we can't help but explore.

Echoes of Brilliance

Bright bulbs flicker on a string,
Mice in tuxedos serenade and sing.
Dancing shadows on the wall,
A disco party for one and all.

Juggling pinecones, tricky and fun,
Under the gaze of the warm sun.
Giddy whispers fill the air,
Even the trees begin to stare.

Ticklish laughter that leaps and hops,
Sprinkler showers that make us stop.
Skipping stones with a funny plop,
Every splash makes the giggles hop.

So gather round, let's laugh till we cry,
With stories ridiculous, oh my, oh my!
In the echoes of this jubilant night,
We find our joy, shining so bright.

Illuminated Paths

Glow sticks wiggle on the floor,
As we giggle and beg for more.
Moonbeams dance upon our heads,
While shadows play in cozy beds.

The streets are lined with sparkly lights,
A parade of silliness ignites.
Marshmallow clouds float by so soft,
As we bounce with laughter aloft.

Every step holds a crunchy crunch,
As we munch and munch during lunch.
The ducks in hats waddle along,
Their quacks harmonize in a silly song.

With every twist and every turn,
We find new ways our hearts can yearn.
So let's stroll on this wondrous quest,
In paths illuminated, we are blessed.

Songs of the Sunflower

In fields where sunflowers dance and play,
They giggle as the wind comes to sway.
With faces bright, they wave so high,
As bees buzz by, oh me, oh my!

They wear tall hats, so proud and bold,
Revealing secrets that never grow old.
They'll sing a tune of yellow delight,
And twirl 'round under the warm moonlight.

The grass beneath them tells silly tales,
Of ladybugs on skateboard trails.
With roots so deep, they're never shy,
Sunflower jokes? You'll laugh and cry!

So come and join this merry band,
Where flowers dream and hope is planned.
In every petal, a smile's found,
In this wild, blooming, happy ground.

Enchanted Horizons

On hills where giggles float like clouds,
Children chase the sun, shouting aloud.
With kites that dance at heights so grand,
They soar through skies like a marching band.

A rabbit hops with a silly flair,
Dancing through grass without a care.
He wears a bowtie, both bright and bold,
Telling stories the world has told.

The mountains chuckle, their peaks so sly,
Winking at clouds that drift on by.
While rivers snicker, they bubble and flow,
Sprinkling delight wherever they go.

So let's sing songs under skies so wide,
Where joy and laughter take us for a ride.
In this magical realm, we'll sway and prance,
As we join in the great cosmic dance.

Chasing Sunbeams

With giggles and glee, we dash and weave,
Chasing those golden rays, we believe.
They slip through our fingers like melted ice,
And tickle our noses like sugar and spice.

A kitten joins in, all fuzzy and spry,
Leaping for shadows that flit as they fly.
With a pounce and a roll, oh what a sight,
It's a furry ballet in the soft warm light!

The sun plays peek-a-boo, so sly and sweet,
Hiding behind clouds, slipping off our feet.
But with every chase, we find new delight,
In the game of light, oh what a bright flight!

So let's race the sunset on this fine day,
With giggles and joy leading the way.
For in every sunbeam that we embrace,
Lies a moment of magic, a warm, radiant space.

Colors of Serenity

In a world where crayons laugh and sing,
They scribble the joy that each day can bring.
With reds and blues that wiggle and sway,
Creating rainbows to brighten our play.

The trees join in, their leaves a-glow,
Shaking with laughter in a breezy flow.
And flowers wink in their vibrant attire,
Painting the garden with giggles of fire.

Butterflies flit in their polka-dot socks,
Dancing with laughter 'round trees like clocks.
Each flutter a jest in this colorful scene,
Where joy and laughter weave through the green.

So come, grab a crayon and color your heart,
In this whimsical world, let's make our art.
For in hues of happiness, we boldly reside,
In the palette of wonder, where smiles collide.

Nature's Canvas of Joy

In fields where daisies dance and twirl,
A squirrel tries to impress a girl.
With acorn hats and silly spins,
He cracks a joke, the laughter begins.

The trees wear hats, the clouds sing low,
As butterflies steal the nature show.
With paintbrush tails, they sweep the air,
In bright confetti—oh, what a flair!

The brook throws giggles, splashes of cheer,
As frogs croak puns for all to hear.
Each blade of grass has a funny name,
In this joyful place, it's all a game!

So laugh with flowers, sway with the breeze,
Join in the play, dance with the bees!
In this bright world where whimsy blends,
Nature's humor never ends!

Petals Paved with Light

The roses wear pajamas, it's true,
In shades of pink, they dance for you.
While lilacs sip on morning tea,
Chattering softly, quite happily.

Sunflowers wear glasses, look so wise,
Reading the clouds, discussing the skies.
While poppies giggle in silken gowns,
Tickling the butterflies, wearing frowns.

Dandelions blow wishes, sprinkled in jest,
Making wishes for a cozy nest.
With each little seed that floats away,
A joke is told to brighten the day!

So stroll through the petals, feel the delight,
In this garden where sparks shine bright.
Each flower whispers a playful tale,
On petals paved with joy, we set sail!

The Enchantment Within

There's magic hiding in the leaves,
A giggle hiding 'neath the eaves.
The mushrooms wear tiny fancy hats,
While ants parade in boots and spats!

The trees tell stories with rustling leaves,
Each secret whispered, nobody believes.
A fox in a cloak, oh what a sight,
Promising everyone magic tonight!

The moon plays pranks with twinkling stars,
Chasing shadows on Earth like cars.
Each beam of light gives a playful poke,
Inviting laughter with every joke.

So wander the woods where laughter's spun,
In the heart of nature, there's endless fun.
With each rustle and shimmer, feel the thrill,
For joy is the magic that time can't still!

Glistening Reflections

At dawn, the dew has jokes to share,
Water droplets in a funny stare.
They wink at flowers who laugh with glee,
As light dances on the busy bee!

The river's mirror holds a sunny grin,
While fish play tag and the otters spin.
They splash and giggle, creating a scene,
In this water wonderland, oh so keen!

The pond throws ripples that tease and play,
Holding the sun like a child's bouquet.
Each splash and shimmer brings joy anew,
Creating smiles in every hue!

So watch the reflections, let laughter sway,
In this glistening world where light holds sway.
As nature chuckles, let's all unite,
In moments of joy, forever bright!

Sunkissed Whispers

Sunshine giggles in the breeze,
Tickling the leaves with such ease.
Grass blades dance, so sprightly bright,
Even the ants are feeling light!

Clouds play hide and seek up high,
As butterflies flaunt, oh my, oh my!
Flowers wink in colors bold,
While bees wear hats of marigold.

Giddy frogs on lilypad thrones,
Croak jokes in ribbits, not in groans.
The sun's a comedian, can't you see?
Laughing with shadows, so merry and free!

So let's skip along the sunlit trail,
With giggles as our only sail.
Chasing giggles that take flight,
In whispers of a warm daylight!

Embracing the Glow

The glow of laughter fills the air,
While squirrels scamper without a care.
Giddy gnomes in gardens dance,
Wiggling their toes, giving chance a chance.

Sunbeams sprinkle like confetti bright,
While daisies sigh in pure delight.
Even the sun grins ear to ear,
As shadows frolic without fear.

Puddles mirror smiles galore,
As puddle jumpers come ashore.
We giggle as we splash and play,
In this melting pot of golden day.

With flowers chatting in their beds,
And chatterbugs spinning crazy threads.
The world's a stage with no tightrope,
Just laughter's song and joy's bright hope!

Nature's Brilliant Palette

Crayons tangled in the trees,
Drawing hues on gentle breeze.
Bubbles float with giggles within,
Nature's palette makes me grin!

The daisies wear their polka dots,
While trees throw shade at all the tots.
Bees are busy making honey,
While flowers tease them saying, "Funny!"

The sun slips on its rainbow cape,
Looking for a brand-new shape.
Colorful socks on grass sprout cheer,
As butterflies join the party here.

Let's paint the day with laughter's brush,
In swirling hues that make us hush.
Oh, vibrant life, you make me see,
Adventure's art, so wild and free!

Daydreams in Bloom

Daydreams dance like petals twirl,
Under the sun, watch them swirl.
Clouds gossip about the sky,
As daffodils flicker an eager eye.

Whimsical wishes float on by,
Riding rainbows from A to Z, oh my!
The twinkling stars, oh what a sight,
Making giggles kiss the night.

Pine trees chuckle, their needles sway,
Nature's laughter leads the way.
With echoes of joy and playful grins,
Let's spin the tales of where it begins.

So while the world wraps us in cheer,
Let's share a hug with the flora near.
In silly dreams, we find our place,
In this bloom of giggles and grace!

Flickers of Hope

The sun peeks out, a shy hello,
The flowers laugh, putting on a show.
Remember the ice cream's crazy swirl,
It melts too fast, watch it twirl!

Rain boots splashing, puddles abound,
Dancing in circles, we leap and bound.
A dog runs by in a bright red cape,
'Super pup!' we cheer, our hero in shape!

The trees tell jokes in the afternoon light,
A squirrel giggles, oh what a sight!
With popsicle sticks and wobbly legs,
We build a castle, on laughter it begs!

In this odd mix of giggles and grins,
Hope flickers on, that's where it begins.
So let's chalk our dreams on this sidewalk so bright,
A canvas of joy, our hearts take flight!

Celestial Serenade

Stars jiggle wildly like popcorn in heat,
The moon croons softly a silly sweet beat.
Aliens peek from behind their green doors,
As comets play tag with cosmic chores!

Dancing on rooftops in mismatched socks,
We moonwalk 'round like zany clocks.
With constellations as our nighttime friends,
We giggle all evening, let laughter extend!

Twinkling dreams in a star-studded race,
While gravity teases, we drift, we embrace.
A comet's a tail, and we're all costume folks,
Dressed as our dreams, we laugh 'til we croak!

So sing to the skies in our silly parade,
With glitter and giggles, memories made.
The universe chuckles, it's all quite absurd,
Yet in all of this laughter, our joy's never blurred!

Awakening in Color

Crayons awaken in vibrant hues,
Painting the world with their wild muse.
Outside the window, a rainbow's a clown,
Dressing the sky in a polka dot gown!

Butterflies flutter, wearing zesty flair,
A snail in sunglasses, without a care.
Spinach sings loudly, "Eat me if you dare!"
While broccoli bubbles, grinning with flair!

Birds at a disco, all flapping their wings,
While daisies in tutus pratfall and sing.
Each sound is a giggle, each color a joke,
As nature produces a whimsical cloak!

So let's paint our lives in a frantic spree,
With giggles and colors, just you and me.
For in this great canvas, so vivid, so bright,
We'll dance through our days in sheer delight!

Radiant Journeys

With each sunrise, a tickle of rays,
The earth whispers secrets in sunlit ballet.
Socks and sandals, a fashion faux pas,
Yet we strut our stuff with an ah-ha!

On bicycles buzzing, bells ringing clear,
We zoom through the streets full of giggly cheer.
A cat on a skateboard gives us a grin,
Watch out, world, we're ready to spin!

Lemonade stands run by cunning young sprites,
Who charge with confetti for sips full of bites.
With pies in the face and a silly old chase,
Our laughter wraps around us in warm, bright lace!

So grab your hats, let's embark on this spree,
With a sprinkle of fun, just you and me.
Each journey we take is a spark of delight,
In the dance of our lives, everything feels right!

The Magic in Bloom

Petals giggle in the breeze,
Bees buzzing with a tease.
Flowers wiggle, dance in arrays,
Bumblebees chant in silly ways.

Colors splash like children play,
In this garden, laughter stays.
Butterflies wear fancy hats,
While the grasshoppers tease the cats.

Sunshine spills like lemonade,
Over petals they parade.
Nature's prank, a playful jest,
Who knew blooms could be so blessed?

With each stem, a secret shared,
Floral giggles, none are scared.
In this patch, the joy's a party,
Join the fun, it's quite hearty!

Radiance Unveiled

Light spills out like jolly jest,
While shadows dance their very best.
The sun plays peek-a-boo with trees,
Whispering secrets with the breeze.

Lampshades wobble with delight,
On each corner, shadows fight.
Laughter echoes in the air,
As light winks without a care.

Squirrels sport their shiny fins,
As they scamper, gather wins.
Glowworms wear their glittering capes,
Making jokes while the world gapes.

From dawn's blush to twilight's hug,
Every giggle's a cozy shrug.
What a scene, a sparkling show,
In the glow, where joy will grow!

Glimmers Beneath the Canopy

Underneath the leafy play,
Where the critters laugh and sway.
Squirrels drop their acorn jokes,
While the grass hums, "What do you hoax?"

Sunbeams sneak like playful spies,
Tickling toes and watchful eyes.
The owls hoot their quirky rhymes,
Counting stars—their silly crimes.

Fireflies wink like cheeky friends,
Their giggles echo as light blends.
Roots and vines weave laughter tight,
Under canopies, what a sight!

Nature's choir sings and beams,
While shadows pull the silliest schemes.
Each rustling leaf holds stories spun,
In this world, it's all in fun!

Dancing with Fireflies

Tiny sparks in twilight's sway,
Fireflies come out to play.
Twinkling tender, they take flight,
Shooting jokes into the night.

They bounce and bob like little sprites,
Crafting giggles from delights.
Each glow is like a laugh released,
In this game, all worries ceased.

The crickets join with chirp and cheer,
Inviting all their friends to near.
Under stars, mischief glows,
As the moon dangles and throws.

Join the dance, don't be shy,
As the light begins to fly.
In this frolic, we unite,
Let's all celebrate the night!

The Lullaby of Spring

The crocuses poke through mud,
They giggle at the cold and bud.
The bees wear tiny hats of gold,
And dance in circles, brave and bold.

Daffodils laugh, their heads held high,
Telling jokes to the passing sky.
A worm in a bowtie wriggles with glee,
Daring a snail to race with a bee.

The rain drops tap on window sills,
Like little drummers sharing thrills.
Puddles form, splashes abound,
As kids jump in with joyful sound.

With breezes that tickle, laughter flows,
A kite flies high, a comic show.
In nature's humor, joy ignites,
Springtime dances with all her sights.

Whispers of Radiance

The morning sun peeks through the trees,
Tickling leaves with playful breeze.
Birds wear sunglasses, chirp a tune,
As squirrels dance under the afternoon.

Butterflies flaunt their vibrant wings,
Twirl like dancers, oh what springs!
A ladybug jigs upon a flower,
Giggling softly, "I've got the power!"

Clouds parade in fluffy costumes,
Making shapes that lighten gloom.
A rabbit hops, a jester bold,
Wearing a crown that's made of gold.

In every corner, laughter spreads,
As nature whispers, teasing threads.
Radiance glimmers, smiles unite,
A whimsical day, pure delight!

Sunlit Reveries

Sunbeams sneak through window panes,
Chasing shadows from the lanes.
Kids in shorts, one sock askew,
Giggle and tumble, what a view!

A cat in a hat lounges in style,
Striking poses, adding a smile.
Birds debate on who can sing best,
While ants march on, an unending quest.

The lemonade stands gleam and shine,
Sipping sweetness, feeling divine.
Laughter echoes in the park,
As twilight hugs the day till dark.

With dreams unfolding in golden light,
Every moment feels just right.
In sunlit glories, joy takes flight,
A playful serenade ignites the night.

Glimmers of Tomorrow

Stars twinkle like they're winking down,
The moon wears a hat, not a frown.
As fireflies play a game of chase,
Glowing bright in this magical space.

Children whisper of dreams to be,
While giggling softly beneath a tree.
A rabbit hops in oversized shoes,
Joined by a fox with fancy hues.

Tomorrow sparkles like a new coin,
Each wish made feels like a rejoicing join.
With hope as our guide, we gladly roam,
In this funny world, we all feel home.

The laughter rolls like waves on sand,
Glimmers of joy at every hand.
In the light of dawn, all is clear,
Tomorrow awaits, let's dance, my dear!

Laughter in the Breeze

Whispers of giggles float in the air,
Squirrels in jackets, like they don't care!
Trees dance around, their leaves cha-cha,
While butterflies laugh, saying, 'Ha-ha!'

Sunbeams bounce, making shadows play,
A dog in a tutu runs on his way!
With clouds forming hats, so silly and round,
Nature's own circus, pure joy to be found.

Birds tell jokes with their chirpy delight,
A waltzing bee, what a silly sight!
Grasshoppers croon their tuneful ballet,
As flowers snap selfies to brighten the day.

The wind tells tales of bright color schemes,
With giggling rainbows and sparkling beams!
In this cheeky world, laughter takes flight,
Every moment bursts with pure, silly light.

The Splendor of New Beginnings

Tiny buds pop, they're having a blast,
Giggling as winter slips by, fast!
With bunnies in bowties and birds in coats,
Spring's snappy entrance, oh, isn't it float?

Daffodils honk with their bright-colored glee,
As warm sunshine tickles the old, wise tree.
Rain drops like confetti, a party to start,
All nature joins in, oh, what a heart!

Grass spruces up in a trendy new green,
While frogs jump in puddles, a wobbly scene.
Every sprout giggles, each leaf gives a wink,
As joy explodes brighter than you might think.

The sun throws glitter, the clouds wear a grin,
The earth's a big stage, let the fun begin!
With whispers of promise, new tales to weave,
In this realm of laughter, we're never naive.

Sparked Afternoons

Picnics on blankets, with ants in a row,
Sandwiches dance like they've stolen the show!
Lemonade rivers flow through our minds,
As squirrels make jokes, oh how time unwinds!

Kites soar high with a tickle and tease,
A wind that chuckles, puts us at ease.
Chasing our shadows, we play hide and seek,
While a butterfly's joke makes us giggle and squeak.

Sunset's a painter with colors so bold,
Each streak a punchline, a story retold.
With laughter like bubbles, our voices take flight,
In these sparked afternoons, oh what a delight!

Chilling in hammocks, we rock and we sway,
Sharing our dreams in a silly way.
Every tick of the clock feels like a cheer,
In this joyous moment, we always hold dear.

Hidden Gardens of Light

Daisies wear glasses, they're reading a book,
While gnomes snap selfies, just take a look!
Sunlight tickles leaves that shimmer and glow,
In hidden gardens where mischief will flow.

Ladybugs prance, dressed up for a ball,
They tango on petals, and there's room for all.
The soil whispers secrets, it's giggling too,
As roots tell tales of the flowers they grew.

Crickets compose a symphony sweet,
As frogs sing their hearts out, what a real treat!
With every soft bloom, there's laughter and mirth,
In these cheerful corners of bright, playful earth.

The moon has a hat made of twinkling stars,
Oh, what a party, let's dance near Mars!
In secretive spots where joy is the theme,
Hidden gardens of light, life is a dream!

The Promise of Bloom

In the garden, blooms pop, a silly sight,
Daisies dance around, feeling quite light.
A tulip trips over its own pretty shoe,
While butterflies giggle, singing 'scoo-bee-doo.'

The bees zoom around, wearing tiny hats,
Buzzing like they're friendly chatterbox brats.
Roses twirl like ballerinas in flight,
While the sun gives a wink, what a funny sight!

Worms in the soil do a conga line cheer,
Telling the daisies, 'We'll always be near.'
Even the carrots, with their green frizzy crown,
Snicker at onions with their layers of frown.

So let's sip some nectar, full of sweet cheer,
Laughing with flowers, it's the best time of year.
With petals and puns, our hearts start to bloom,
As smiles sprout wildly, erasing all gloom.

Mornings Wrapped in Gold

Waking up to toast with a golden glow,
Butterflies yawn, moving ever so slow.
The sun spills its laughter on sleepy-eyed trees,
While birds crack jokes in the cool, morning breeze.

Pancakes stack high, like a tower so neat,
Syrup slides down, a sweet sticky treat.
A squirrel, quite bold, takes a leap for his prize,
Shimmies on branches, a clown in disguise.

Jellybeans bounce on the bright morning grass,
Frogs join the chorus, with a leap and a sass.
The sky chuckles softly, tickled by light,
While shadows wear smiles in a playful delight.

With giggles and snippets of pure, sunny cheer,
Mornings in gold bring the world near and dear.
So raise up a mug filled with laughter and cheer,
And toast to those mornings that twinkle with cheer!

Magic Beneath the Sky

Under a canvas of deep blue so wide,
Clouds dressed in fluff let their giggles reside.
A kite takes a dive, then tumbles about,
With whispers of wind echoing laughter and shout.

Stars peek at the earth, like winking kids,
'Is that a friendly owl or a raccoon with fibs?'
The moon plays hide-and-seek with a star,
Chasing one another—in a dance from afar.

Fireflies flutter with their twinkling lights,
Winking at folks who've finished their nights.
Crickets strum tunes on their tiny, loud legs,
While the world chuckles on, like a mother who begs.

So gather your friends, let's revel till dawn,
In the magic that hums, from dusk until dawn.
With laughter like stardust in the cool of the night,
Let joy paint our souls with colors so bright.

Twilight's Gentle Embrace

As twilight wraps the world in a fluffy shawl,
Fireflies twinkle, having a lovely ball.
The crickets recite their melodious rhymes,
While the sun giggles, saying, 'I'll be back in no time!'

A cat struts by, with a self-satisfied grin,
Watching the night take a gentle spin.
Squirrels nestle in, wrapping tails tight,
Whispering secrets to the soft, fading light.

In shadows, a joke travels from tree to tree,
As oak chuckles softly, 'Come join the spree!'
The breeze brings a message, oh so coy,
'Let's dance 'neath the stars and spread all the joy.'

So toast to the evening, with a grin so wide,
In twilight's soft arms, let laughter abide.
With whimsy and giggles, the world feels so sane,
In the sprinkle of dusk, we laugh without strain.

Chasing the Daybreak

In pajamas, I sprint, feeling so spry,
A squirrel steals my toast, oh my oh my!
The rooster's a comedian, loud and bright,
Dreams fade with sunlight, just out of sight.

Chasing the sun, we trip on our shoes,
With giggles galore, we laugh at our blues.
Butterflies flutter, join in our spree,
As we sing to the clouds, 'Look at me!'

A cat in a hat gives a wink with a grin,
It juggles our breakfast; let the fun begin!
The honeybee dances, it's such a delight,
As we chase the dawn, oh, what a sight!

Hats made of foil, we wear with great flair,
Nonsense and joy hang thick in the air.
With each goofy step, the world feels so right,
We're the jesters today in this whimsical light.

Luminous Dreams

The moon sneezed, a bright shimmer ignites,
Stars chuckle and scatter, what quirky sights!
I float on a cloud made of marshmallow fluff,
Encouraged by giggles, the night's never tough.

A dream of a dragon, it's wearing my shoes,
While fairies dine on popcorn, oh, what a ruse!
They spread sparkling laughter wrapped round in delight,
I join in their dance, twirling left and right.

A pickle with glasses recites silly rhymes,
As teacups do ballet, oh, how they chime!
We toast with our spoons to the new morning light,
Our laughter echoes, pure joy in full flight.

When dawn finally calls, I refuse to depart,
Still savoring magic, I hold it close to my heart.
With luminous echoes, I step out in cheer,
Knowing each silly dream will soon reappear.

The Dance of Dawn

A chicken in heels struts, so sassy and spry,
With pom-poms of feathers, it waves and says hi!
We twirl with the daisies, in dew-soaked ballet,
As laughter spills over, brightening the day.

The sun winks at us, throws an impish grin,
While frogs in tuxedos join in with a spin.
Hopping and flopping, we swing to the beat,
In this dance of dawn, life feels so sweet.

A mischievous breeze tosses hair in a whirl,
While the petals of flowers in delight start to twirl.
We slide on the grass, free-spirited and bold,
Embracing the moment as stories unfold.

With butterflies leading, we spin through the air,
In this zany parade, there's laughter to share.
So come, join the fun, let your worries be gone,
For this dance of dawn is where we belong!

Shimmers in Twilight

In the twilight glow, fireflies buzz and tease,
They dance like they're tipsy, with such carefree ease.
We trip on our shadows, laugh loud and wild,
As the stars join in, twinkling like a child.

A raccoon with a top hat takes a comical bow,
While bats serenade us, somehow, someway—wow!
The moon plays the trumpet, as crickets tap dance,
In this silly encore, we're caught in a trance.

Chocolate chip cookies float by on parade,
With sprinkles and laughter, delightful cascade.
As we gather the shimmers, in joy we imbibe,
This playful horizon ignites our wild vibe.

So let's make a toast to these twilight delights,
With giggles and shadows, let's dance through the nights.

For while we may stumble, we're wrapped up in cheer,
In this crazy old journey, we've nothing to fear.

When Dreams Take Flight

In slippers soft, we soar quite high,
Chasing squirrels that dance and fly.
With mismatched socks and hats askew,
We paint the sky in shades of blue.

Unicorns prance in fields of cheese,
While jellybeans float like autumn leaves.
A napkin hat atop my head,
I giggle loud as dreams unfold in bed.

Our pet goldfish dons a cape so bright,
Saves the world from pizza plight.
As laughter echoes through the night,
We drift on clouds of pure delight.

So when the moon begins to peek,
We frolic on the joy that we seek.
With every dream, both silly and true,
We find the magic in all we do.

A Dance of Radiant Shadows

Bouncing cats in pointy shoes,
Twirl with mice that sing the blues.
Shadows giggle, play a game,
While the moon shouts out my name.

Dancing with a broomstick's sway,
As broomsticks sashay, what a play!
Cupcakes waltz across the floor,
While silly ghosts knock on the door.

Jellyfish in top hats spin,
As donuts cheer the fun we're in.
The trees sway in a funny trance,
Twirling leaves join in the dance.

And when the dawn begins to break,
The shadows laugh, oh what a quake!
For every step we take tonight,
Was just a jest of sheer delight.

Moments of Celestial Clarity

Stars with socks hang in the air,
Wobble with a giggling flair.
Planets toss confetti bright,
While comets call to join the flight.

Galaxies hum a silly tune,
To tickle hearts with cosmic swoon.
As asteroids play hopscotch near,
I can't resist, I disappear.

Lunar llamas jump with glee,
Leaping high above the sea.
With every twinkle, chuckles rise,
In the vast and jolly skies.

So let us soar on giggles bold,
In the universe, bright and gold.
For every twinkling star we see,
Is a wink of joy, just for thee.

Rays of the Heart

Sunbeams tickle my silly nose,
As laughter blooms like a garden rose.
With donuts spinning on each ray,
I find a smile that's here to stay.

Balloons chat and share their dreams,
While chocolate rivers flow with gleams.
Each giggle dances in the air,
Bringing joy beyond compare.

Waffles play hopscotch on the grass,
As rabbits cheer, oh what a blast!
The breeze is chuckling in delight,
With every glance, the world feels bright.

And as the day slips into night,
Fireflies flash their wondrous light.
For in our hearts, we feel the spark,
Of laughter's glow, both bright and dark.

Dappled Sunlight

Sunbeams dance on the ground,
Like socks tossed all around.
Giggles rise with each beam,
In a world where silly's the theme.

Frogs wear shades, so chic and nifty,
While squirrels raid gardens, feeling shifty.
Flowers wink, each petal a joke,
Nature chuckles, her laughter bespoke.

Bees buzzing like they're on a spree,
Chasing butterflies, as happy as can be.
Every ray a playful cue,
Let's frolic, the sun's in the mood!

So grab a friend, frolic and twirl,
In dappled dreams, let laughter unfurl.
For sunshine is a giddy delight,
Bringing joy from morning till night.

Whirlwind of Color

Pinks and yellows swirl about,
Marigolds dance, no hint of doubt.
Lemons laugh on the citrus trees,
While rainbows tease on the lightest breeze.

Tulips in tutus, striking a pose,
Daffodils shimmy, spilling their prose.
Petunias clapping in vibrant cheer,
While daisies joke, "We're all here!"

A bluebird carries a tiny hat,
Winking at a very silly cat.
Hummingbirds buzz like little spies,
In this color storm, laughter flies!

So spin with joy, let colors collide,
With nature's palette, let's not hide.
In this riot of hues, we'll find our song,
Where laughter and color can't go wrong!

Radiance in Each Step

With each small step, glitter rains down,
Sidewalks sparkle; oh, what a town!
Every puddle reflects a grin,
As giggles echo where we've been.

Sidewalk chalk draws laugh-out-loud,
A scribble parade, colorful and proud.
Jump in a splash, a quick little dance,
In this radiant world, give joy a chance!

Umbrellas bloom like flowers in spring,
Bouncing along on the joy they bring.
Footprints sparkle with silly glee,
As laughter tiptoes, wild and free.

So tie your shoes, let mischief unfold,
With radiant steps, be joyful and bold.
In this giggle-filled journey, run wild,
With each hop and skip, unleash your inner child!

Light's Sweet Embrace

Cuddled close by golden rays,
Sunshine hugs in a million ways.
A butterfly lands on a child's nose,
Tickling laughter where the sunlight glows.

Chirping crickets throw a party in trees,
Singing silly songs in the upcoming breeze.
Fireflies twinkle with cheeky delight,
Winking at us, saying 'Stay all night!'

In this embrace, shadows play,
As the sun winks and ticks away.
A rabbit hops, wearing sunglasses proud,
In light's warm hug, we are all allowed.

So twirl and bask in this glowing grace,
Join the fun; it's a magical place.
For in every giggle, in every cheer,
Light's sweet embrace brings smiles near!

Serenade of the Sunbeams

The sunbeams dance like bumblebees,
Tickling noses in the gentle breeze.
They beam and grin, a cheeky lot,
Turning the grumpy into a happy spot.

Butterflies in bow ties prance,
They twirl and swirl in a silly dance.
Their colors clash, a chaotic spree,
Who knew bright hues could make you flee?

Squirrels wear sunglasses, quite the sight,
Holding acorns like they own the night.
They gossip 'round the tree trunk stout,
Oh, the stories stars could shout!

So here's to joy in daft array,
Let's bask in laughter every day.
With silly songs and carefree cheer,
These sunny moments we hold dear!

Marvels in the Meadow

In the meadow, grasshoppers sing,
Their tiny voices—what joy they bring!
With legs like springs, they jump so high,
I swear they're lost in the blue sky.

Daisies gossip with the dandelions,
Whispering secrets as the sun aligns.
"Did you see that bee? So bold, so brash!"
It's buzzing drama, a meadow flash!

Caterpillars sashay, decked in fuzz,
Pretending they're royalty, all because.
They strut their stuff, it's quite the show,
But who knew butterflies were so in the know?

As evening falls, the fireflies blink,
In their little dance, they hardly think.
Light up the night! They twinkle and glow,
A giggling fanfare, putting on a show!

Flickers of Hope

Little stars in the sky share jokes,
"We're just bright dots, not silly folks!"
They giggle and twinkle, such a sight,
Whispering puns to the moon at night.

The owls, wise with their grand old tales,
Chime in with hoots as the wind exhales.
"Whooo's there?" they ask in a voice so deep,
As crickets croak secrets meant for sleep.

The dusk paints giggles across the ground,
As shadows stretch and dance around.
With every flicker of laughter near,
Hope's little sparks ignite our cheer!

So let's not fret about the dark,
For even shadows can leave a mark.
In the glow of joy, let's always be,
Finding the light in simplicity!

Blossoms in the Breeze

Petals swirl like confetti in the air,
Just blooming flowers trying to flare.
They giggle, toss their heads with grace,
"Who wore it best?"—what a silly race!

The trees tell tales as old as time,
Whispering secrets, creating rhyme.
With roots that wiggle and branches that sway,
If trees could laugh, they'd shout hooray!

Breezes play tag, they push and pull,
Turning quiet days into something full.
"Catch me if you can!" they softly tease,
As sunlit giggles dance through the leaves.

Let's toast to blooms, a carefree things,
To laughter found in the tiniest springs.
In the playful world, let's take a chance,
And twirl with joy in nature's dance!

The Colorful Embrace of Twilight

As evening paints the sky in flair,
The squirrels dance and giggle in air.
With winks from stars, they play tag,
Chasing moonbeams, in night's wag.

Laughter bubbles from below,
Where shadows stretch and twist like dough.
The fireflies blink, a quirky show,
While willows sway to the breezy flow.

Clouds wear hats of pink and gold,
Whispering secrets, stories untold.
As crickets serenade the night,
The world chuckles, oh, what a sight!

Beneath this sky, whimsical and bright,
The oddball creatures take their flight.
In playful mischief, they unite,
As twilight welcomes joy with delight.

Awakening of the Horizon

A sleepy sun yawns with a grin,
Stretches wide, letting the day begin.
Penguins in bow ties race for their treats,
While roosters try on fancy feats.

The flowers wiggle, tickled by rays,
Doing the cha-cha in cheerful displays.
Bees in tuxedos buzz on parade,
Gathering nectar in a sweet charade.

Clouds puff up, all fluffy and bright,
Playing peek-a-boo, what a delight!
The horizon giggles, stretching its bounds,
As laughter echoes all around.

A parade of colors marches with cheer,
Where every critter brings laughter near.
Oh, the joy as the day unfolds,
In this playful world, a wonder untold.

Echoes of the Enchanted

In the forest, where whispers play,
Trees gossip giggles in their leafy sway.
Mice tell tales of their daring quests,
While owls wear spectacles, all dressed.

A brook chuckles, tickling the stones,
Echoing laughter in lilting tones.
A raccoon juggles acorns with flair,
As fireflies dance in the evening air.

Dragons napped on the hills so steep,
Woke with a grin, they couldn't keep.
They fluffed their wings, ready for fun,
And grooved to a beat under the sun.

Oh, what a party with mischief and glee,
In the echo of laughter, wild and free.
Under stars that twinkle like little sprites,
The enchanted night, oh, what delights!

Twilight's Gentle Embrace

As sundown tiptoes on tippy toes,
Balloons float by with a giggle and pose.
Bunnies wear shades, sipping their tea,
While shadows chuckle, 'Oh, let it be!'

The stars throw confetti from up above,
Winking at snails who scoot with love.
A dance of the silly, where all things twirl,
As the moon casts smiles on each little swirl.

With whispers of twilight, a playful tease,
The breeze sprinkles laughter on giddy trees.
The world's a playground, a stage so bright,
Where silliness reigns in the soft fading light.

So join the frolic, let spirits take flight,
In this realm of wonder, all feels just right.
In twilight's embrace, joy takes its place,
As giggles take over, a timeless grace.

A Tapestry of Radiance

The sun woke up with a yawn,
Stretching its rays on the lawn.
A squirrel danced in a hat too big,
While bees buzzed tunes, doing a jig.

The grass giggled with morning dew,
As flowers painted a bright debut.
A dog tried to catch a butterfly,
And ended up slipping in pie, oh my!

Clouds wore shoes of fluffy white,
Jumping around, what a sight!
A gust of wind played tag with the trees,
Whispering secrets to the buzzing bees.

As day danced on with silly grace,
Laughter echoed, lighting up the place.
With every twist and every turn,
Life's little quirks made hearts just burn.

The Symphony of Spheres

Planets spun in a playful race,
Stars twinkled with a mischievous face.
A comet slipped on a cosmic slide,
Shooting candy across the sky wide.

The moon chuckled, dressed in cheese,
While meteors wiggled in the breeze.
Galaxies wobbled, trying to keep pace,
With a symphony of giggles, a laughing space.

Saturn's rings jiggled with glee,
While Jupiter sang off-key, you see.
A black hole grinned, said 'Join the fun!',
As aliens danced; they knew how to run.

In this grand laughter of glowing night,
Each twinkling star added sheer delight.
With cosmic pranks and interstellar cheers,
The universe played on, banishing fears.

Moonlit Serenades

At night the moon wore a silly grin,
Casting light where shadows had been.
Owls held concerts with hoots of glee,
As crickets fiddled under the tree.

Fireflies twinkled like tiny lights,
Dancing around in whimsical flights.
A raccoon band played on a log,
While foxes waltzed with a happy dog.

Stars joined in, all dressed to impress,
Singing sweet tunes, causing a mess.
A cloud came by, carrying a tune,
Swaying gently, the night was a boon.

As laughter echoed, the night took flight,
Mysteries faded with joy in sight.
In a serenade under skies so bright,
Every heart knew what pure fun feels like.

Beyond the Veil of Day

As day gave way to a jolly eve,
The sun hid behind with tricks up its sleeve.
A rainbow slipped on its vibrant socks,
And danced with glee atop the rocks.

Breezes giggled as colors swirled,
While butterflies twirled and twirled.
The trees pulled faces, swaying side to side,
In a game of tag where joy can't hide.

Sunset chimed with colors so bright,
Capturing laughter, painting the night.
Stars peeked in, promoted as best,
In a lineup of smiles, they stood out from the rest.

So beyond day's veil, with whimsical heights,
Every moment sparkled, full of delights.
Laughter and joy ran wild and free,
In a world where wonder is easy to see.

The Glow of Adventure

Bouncing off the walls with glee,
Chasing shadows, can you see?
With giggles spilling everywhere,
We leap and twirl without a care.

Bugs wear hats, they take a stand,
Fish in ponds have formed a band.
Trees do dances, leaves applaud,
The world's a stage, how very odd!

Squirrels trade their acorn stash,
Crafting games where truth meets trash.
Racing clouds across the sky,
High-fiving stars as they fly by.

With shiny stones we pave our way,
Today's a game, let's laugh and play!
Through every twist, each silly clue,
Adventure's glow shines bright and true.

,tal Clear Mornings

;pills juice upon the ground,
ist kind of breakfast found.
ls in pajamas start to sing,
Greet the day with everything!

Toasts and jams, they dance and prance,
Butterflies join in the dance.
Coffee brews with fluffy steam,
Mornings feel like a frothy dream.

Pancakes flipping to and fro,
Syrup rivers seem to flow.
Jelly beans jump in delight,
As laughter fills the crystal light.

Chasing sunlight down the street,
Every moment feels so sweet.
With heartbeats racing like a race,
Joyful grins on every face.

Tranquil Brilliance

Stars in pajamas snore with ease,
Moonbeams glow, they love to tease.
Crickets sing a gentle tune,
Nighttime hugs beneath the moon.

Blankets of velvet kiss the sky,
Clouds wear smiles, don't be shy!
Whispers of dreams float through the air,
Wishes dance without a care.

Bugs in jammies read their books,
Imagining all kinds of hooks.
Fireflies glow, like thoughts in flight,
Magic drifts throughout the night.

In a world of soft and bright,
Everyone joins the peaceful light.
With every twinkle, every sigh,
Tranquility makes time fly.

A Canvas of Hope

Colors splash across the sky,
Pinks and yellows making us fly.
A brush of luck, a stroke of cheer,
Painting dreams that feel so near.

Daisies giggle on the ground,
Tickling toes as we jump around.
Rainbows swear they've seen it all,
Chasing puddles, we slip and fall.

Canvas bright with every hue,
Stories told and painted new.
Crayons laughing in a heap,
Dreams awaken from their sleep.

With every stroke, a tale unfolds,
Hope like stories yet untold.
In this world both bright and vast,
Let's create a future that'll last.

Milton Keynes UK
Ingram Content Group UK Ltd.
UKHW021021251124
451242UK00021B/93